reinvent

a small book with a big idea

by chris farrell

TABLE OF CONTENTS

2000 years ago, a teacher called Epictetus asked the question: "*How long are you going to wait until you demand the best of yourself? You are no longer a child; you are a full-grown person. And yet, you procrastinate.*"

Hi.

Chris Farrell here.

This book is in two parts.

Part One: The WHAT

Part Two: The HOW

In part one, we are going to cover **WHAT** you need to do to reinvent your life.

In part two, we will move on to **HOW** to achieve this.

No fluff, no filler. Just actionable content.

Ready...?

WHO IS THIS BOOK FOR?

If you feel you are not everything you could be, this book is for you.

If you feel you are a million miles away from where you thought you would be, this book is for you.

If you want to achieve more in the next six months than you have in the last six years, this book is for you.

REINVENT YOURSELF

Let's just get clear on something.

Life is tough.

I get it.

Everybody is going through something.

However, here's something I want you to think about.

You really are capable of making the biggest transformation of your life.

Despite what you might be thinking.

But to **REALLY** achieve this, you are going to have to **CHANGE.**

Deep down inside, you know this.

Deep down inside you know if you continue to do pretty much the same things day in day out, your life is pretty much going to remain the same, day in day out.

Therefore, all **CHANGE** starts with the understanding that you are going to need to do something **DIFFERENT.**

To put it another way, to create the level of life you ultimately want, you will have to change something (maybe many things) you do daily.

This means you will have to **UNLEARN** old habits.

Are you open to this?

If so, let's continue.

PART ONE:

The WHAT

In the movie Rocketman, a young Elton John asks how he can become a soul singer.

He's told he needs to *'kill the man you are to become the man you want to be.'*

Are you ready to 'kill' the old you to become a new you?

Think about your life right now.

Can you stop dabbling in wanting to improve yourself, and instead really **COMMIT** to it?

Could you do this for one year? Maybe three?

Here's the Good News.

History is riddled with people who have done this, people who have reinvented themselves, and who have gone on to lead a life of meaning.

Here's the Bad News.

We are going to have to re-wire some habitual thoughts and beliefs that you have about yourself.

Ready?

WHAT IF?

ALL GREAT *change* **IS PRECEDED BY** *chaos*

Here's a radical thought.

What if all the struggles you are going through right now are in fact a beautiful **GIFT?**

What if they are exactly what are needed to allow you to become the person you are supposed to be?

I do understand that if you are really struggling and are in a lot of emotional distress and pain right now, this can be difficult concept to consider.

"There is no 'GIFT' in what I am going through!" you say.

You know what the solution is.

It's simple!

You need more money.

Or you need your partner to get their act together.

Or you need that health issue to be resolved.

Or you need to get your home situation sorted.

Or you need to get a well-paid job.

Whatever the thing is that is causing you the most anxiety right now, if that could be solved, well, that's the solution!

That's all that needs to be fixed!

If you can resolve that thing, you will be fine!

Guess what?

You're 100% wrong.

That's not all that needs fixing.

Despite what you may be thinking, the challenges you are experiencing right now **ARE**, in fact, a **BLESSING.**

The challenges you are currently battling with **ARE** exactly what you **NEED** to **FORCE** you to **REALIZE** how **STRONG** you can become (despite how beaten and defeated and hopeless you may be feeling).

The obstacles you are up against right now **ARE** exactly what you **NEED** (however not necessarily what you want) to learn **NEW SKILLS** to become this new you.

A new you?

Feels good, right?

IF IT DOESN'T...

challenge you

IT DOESN'T...

change you

Here's something to ponder.

Steve Jobs said we can only join up the dots in our life looking back.

What this means is, you don't know **RIGHT NOW**, how something that you are dealing with **AT THIS VERY MOMENT** (or trying to deal with) is going to nudge your life in a different direction, resulting in something (or maybe someone) new coming into your life.

A good question to ask yourself is:

> *"Is it possible the challenges in my life right now are here so I can discover what I am capable of?"*

Maybe.

> Seneca said: *"You are unfortunate if you have never lived through misfortune. You have passed through life without an opponent. No one can ever know what you are capable of. Not even you."*

> Rockefeller said: *"Oh, how blessed are those who have to struggle for a foundation in life. I shall never cease to be grateful for the years of struggles and the difficulties to be overcome."*

You are capable of making the biggest transformation of your life.

And here's the thing, significant lasting change does **NOT** take years.

But it **DOES** start with the understanding that you are going to need to do something different from what you are doing now.

To create a life that you ultimately want you will have to **CHANGE** something you do **DAILY**.

The good news is it only takes one skill.

Can you guess what that is?

You got it.

Courage.

COURAGE

If you only take one thing away from this short book let it be this.

The #1 skill to develop is **COURAGE.**

This is so important so let's say it again!

The #1 skill to develop is COURAGE.

COURAGE is the foundation of any type of change.

COURAGE is where all change starts.

You may have heard of the book 'THE TOP FIVE REGRETS of the DYING', by Bronnie Ware.

(Side note: if you haven't read it, just Google and read the blog post).

This is an excellent book (and blog post) written by a palliative nurse who looked after countless patients in the final few weeks of their lives.

Guess what the universal #1 regret of the dying is?

Have a guess? I think you may know…

The Number One Regret of the dying was **NOT having had the COURAGE to live a life true to themselves**.

Think about that.

The #1 Regret, even at their death bed, **MOST** people regretted **NOT** having had the **COURAGE** to live a life true to themselves.

Is this what we want to say about our life?

Is this what you want to say about your life?

LIFE shrinks or expands in proportion to one's courage

I think about the #1 Regret of the Dying every day.

What a gift to have this knowledge shared with us.

We can save 20/30/40+ years of regret by really listening to this powerful revelation and taking it on board.

So, let's say it again!

The #1 Regret, even on their death bed, was **NOT** having had the **COURAGE** to live a life true to themselves.

SIGNIFICANT LASTING *change* DOES NOT TAKE *years*

So, let me ask you question: What is going on in your life right now that you would like to have the courage to change?

There may be many things.

But think about just one.

Worried about money? Health? Battling with depression? Don't like what you see in the mirror? Want out of a relationship? Wasting your time? Addiction? Battling with negative thoughts? Living in the past? Scared of the future? Running out of money? Wasting too much time on YouTube?   Struggling to start that business? Feel too old? Don't know what to do with your life? Comparing yourself to others? Feel like a fraud? Want to start that side hustle, write that book, fix that health challenge? Alcohol, drugs, PTSD? Hiding a mental health issue from everyone? Procrastination, anxiety, stress, body dysmorphia?

Everybody is going through something.

The **ONLY** thing that is stopping you getting started on the path of reinvention is **COURAGE.**

It's time to stop lurking in the shadows.

It's time to stop being the servant when you can be the master.

It's time to start the process to become the person you secretly sense you can be.

The man that finds himself on top of a mountain didn't fall there

Countless people in far worse situations than you are in right now have gone before you and done the same.

Now it's your turn.

Jim Carrey tells a beautiful story about courage.

He talks about his father, and he says that his father could have been a great comedian, but he didn't think it was possible.

So, he made a conservative choice and got a safe job as an accountant.

And when he was 50, he was let go from his job.

Jim learned that you can fail at what you don't want to do...

...so, you might as well take a chance on doing something that you do love.

Remember the #1 REGRET OF THE DYING:

They wished they'd had the COURAGE to live a life true to themselves.

It's time to face your demons, pick up your burdens, and walk up that hill.

Yes, it's going to be scary.

But do know what's even scarier?

Doing nothing, and you and I having this same conversation in five years from now.

WHY MOST PEOPLE DO NOT CHANGE

Here's something worth noting.

Most people do not really change (sure, some do. And we all can. But most don't.).

Why is this?

Simple.

Because CHANGE is painful.

That's why change is so difficult for most people because it means **VOLUNTARILY taking on pain.**

As humans we are not conditioned to do this.

And that is why most people do not change.

Most people choose comfort.

But what makes you comfortable, can kill you.

What makes you uncomfortable, is the only way to grow.

If you do what is easy, your life will be hard.

But if you do what is hard, your life will be easy.

> Pope Benedict XVI said: *"The world promises you comfort, but you were not made for comfort. You were made for greatness."*

> Kahil Gibran in The Prophet says: *"The lust for comfort murders our soul, and then walks grinning to our funeral."*

There are consequences if you seek comfort.

And because most people choose comfort, they do not push themselves.

And I mean **REALLY** push themselves.

It's generally considered that most people are operating at 2% of their capability. I'd suggest it's even lower.

But think about this.

If you are barely hanging in there and you are functioning at 2%, imagine what you could do at 20%!

DON'T
procrastinate

That's 10 times more productive and efficient than you are now - and that only takes you to 20%.

Imagine you can get up to 50%!

And therefore, maybe the struggles and the battles and the depressions and the anxieties in your life right now ARE indeed a **GIFT,** to push us to become the person we are supposed to be.

Just maybe.

The following poem by Guillaume Apollinaire sums this up perfectly.

"Come to the edge," he said.

"We can't, we're afraid!" they responded.

"Come to the edge," he said.

"We can't, we will fall!" they responded.

"Come to the edge," he said.

And so they came.

And he pushed them.

And they flew."

OBSTACLES = GROWTH

The Japanese have an art called Kintsugi.

Kintsugi is fitting broken plates with gold.

The more cracks, the more gold they are filled with.

In the end, the most broken plates became the strongest and the most valuable.

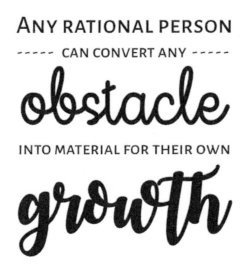

And so it is, the more breaks and cracks you endure, the more golden you become.

In learning to repair ourselves, we can come back bigger, better, and stronger than ever.

So how do we grow?

We grow by voluntarily taking on challenges.

Read that again.

We grow by voluntarily taking on challenges.

Everyone is looking for the elevator to success.

There is no elevator.

You must take the stairs.

We must begin to learn to not only **LOVE** our obstacles…

…but to also realize that they are the only path to growth.

Did you know when Superman first came out in the 1930s, he was instantly loved.

However, something fascinating happened after a few short years.

As Superman became more and more invincible, his comics became more and more unpopular.

Why?

The reason is simple: **a hero with no obstacle is no hero at all.**

People got bored of Superman being unbeatable.

As a result, Superman's story was re-written to include kryptonite, to give the man of steel an obstacle, so the audience could identify.

In Ryan Holiday's excellent book, The Obstacle Is The Way, he writes:

> *"Not many people have trained themselves to see the OPPORTUNITY with obstacles. What befell them is not some unsalvageable misfortune, but the gift of education."*

17

And this really is the secret to a meaningful life.

Every single one of us faces adversity.

It's not because we're unlucky. It's by design.

Life intentionally gives us obstacles.

Read that again.

It's because it knows the path to any growth is through some sort of obstacle.

In other words, life happens **FOR** us, not to us.

We need to therefore learn to recognize the gift that comes with every hurdle.

It's the **challenges** that come our way, that contain within them an opportunity to grow, which lead, ultimately, to happiness.

If you do what is easy,
your life will be hard.
If you do what is hard,
your life will be easy.

3 UNIVERSAL TRUTHS

THAT NOBODY WILL EVER TELL YOU

I'd like to share **3 Universal Truths** that nobody will ever tell you.

These may sound shocking to some, but these **TRUTHS** will save you maybe years of time-wasting if you really understand and implement them.

Ready?

1: NOBODY IS COMING TO SAVE YOU.

Not only is this brutally true, it's also wonderfully refreshing to know.

There is a scene in the spectacular movie Alive that sums this up perfectly.

Alive tells the incredible true story of the harrowing events following a plane crash.

In 1972, a plane carrying 45 passengers, including the Uruguayan rugby team, crashed in the mountains while flying from Uruguay to Chile.

The plane crashed in parts and was scattered on the endless frozen ground.

Stranded and alone, those that survived did all they could to keep warm, look after the injured, while waiting to be rescued.

A few days passed, then a week, before eventually the captain heard on a transistor radio that the search party had been called off.

He returned to his men and gathered them around.

"Good news!" he said, *"the search party has been called off!"*

His men, freezing, hungry and injured did not understand why this was good news.

The captain went onto explain.

"Because this means we're going to get out of here ourselves. We're not going to wait for a search party that may never appear."

Think about that.

"We're not going to wait for a search party that may never appear."

STOP WAITING FOR A

Search
Party

THAT IS NEVER
GOING TO APPEAR

Are you waiting for a search party?

Guess what?

It's never going to appear.

Brutal, right?

But it's also good to know, because deep down inside, I suspect you have sensed this to be true.

> Jim Rohn said: *"If you don't plan your own life, chances are you'll fall into someone else's plans. And guess what they have planned for you? Not much."*

So.

Stop.

Waiting.

You are responsible for your own flourishing.

You.

No one else.

If you are waiting for someone or something to come and save you, you're going to be waiting a long time.

And while we're on this subject matter, here's something else to keep top of mind.

Hardly anyone cares.

Don't make the mistake of thinking because you post something on social media and you get a few comments and likes, that people care.

Guess what, they don't.

Nobody will ever tell you this, so I will.

80% of people don't care what you are going through.

19.99% of people are secretly pleased you are having a tough time.

However, if you are lucky, 0.01% of people will genuinely care.

I realize this is harsh to say, but it's also very freeing, as it underlines what I have said, which is **nobody is coming to save you.**

So, you are in a tough spot right now?

Good.

Because not only are you are going to get out it yourself ...

... but you're also going to become a better version of yourself as a result.

2: LIFE IS SUFFERING. ACCEPT THAT VOLUNTARILY AND YOU ARE TRANSCENDED.

LIFE IS...

Suffering

ACCEPT THAT...

Voluntarily

No tree becomes deep-rooted and sturdy unless strong winds blow against it.

Think about that.

> Seneca once said: *"Why are good men shaken? They are shaken so they can grow back strong."*

Let me ask you, what strong winds are blowing against you at the moment?

You may have health issues.

You may be in a serious financial spot.

You may be an age you don't want to be.

You may feel your life has passed you by.

You may not like who you see in the mirror.

You may be a single parent and alone.

You may be completely alone.

You may have no home.

You may feel you are wasting your life.

You may feel unappreciated.

You may feel you have done nothing in your life in the last 10 years.

You may feel trapped.

You may be procrastinating.

You may be questioning 'how did my life end up like this?'.

As we have already said, everybody is going through something.

NO TREE BECOMES
deep rooted & sturdy
UNLESS STRONG WINDS
blow against it

Everybody gets kicked about a bit.

Life is difficult.

In fact, religious people have been saying this forever.

Life is suffering, they say.

In the Four Noble Truths, which are the essence of Buddha's teachings, the first Noble Truth simply says:

Life is Suffering.

(You may like to know that the Second Noble Truth reveals that suffering comes from desire, and the Third Noble Truth states that suffering ends when we cut off that desire).

So… life is suffering.

Hardly anyone says this.

Particularly in this social media world that we inhabit where everyone is posting filtered pictures of themselves and their 'great' life.

It's liberating to understand that one of the fundamental realities of life, is suffering.

ALL of us are suffering **EVERY DAY** in a multitude of ways, physically, mentally, financially, emotionally.

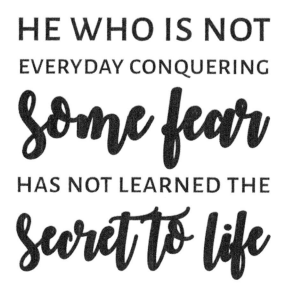

HE WHO IS NOT
EVERYDAY CONQUERING
some fear
HAS NOT LEARNED THE
Secret to life

Life is suffering.

Life is not fair.

We need to get used to this.

However, should life be fair?

Is fairness even a desirable state?

Does fairness challenge you to be creative, to grow, to evolve, to learn, to expand, to reinvent yourself?

Dr Jordan Peterson says: *"even though life is suffering, if you are sufficiently courageous, you'll find that there is something within you that will respond with the development of an ability that will transcend the suffering."*

In other words, if you take people and you expose them voluntarily to things they are avoiding, they get stronger.

You will get stronger.

And we don't know what the upper limit to this is.

If you are religious, C.S. Lewis suggests: *"it's because God loves us, he gave us the gift of suffering."*

In his book Can't Hurt Me, David Goggins says: *"Don't be on that spoon fed path of least resistance.   Your answers are buried in all that suffering."*

The godfather of personal development Jim Rohn said: *'don't wish that things were easier; with that you were better."*

The more we study suffering, the more we realize it contains a hidden opportunity for growth and achievement.

Suffering is an opportunity.

Sure, it hurts, but that doesn't lessen its value.

We need to **GROW** through what we **GO** through.

Remember, while the beauty may be in the butterfly, the growth happens in the cocoon.

It's the struggle to free ourselves that gives us the strength to fly.

Your suffering is your fuel to propel you to greater heights.

Despite what every part of your being may be saying, you **NEED** this suffering.

So don't run from it.

Don't avoid it.

Embrace it.

And you will be transcended.

THE ONE WHO CANNOT
BE UPSET BY ANYTHING
OUTSIDE THEIR CONTROL

3: CHANGE THE WAY YOU LOOK AT THINGS AND THE THINGS YOU LOOK AT CHANGE.

The third Universal Truth is all about having the courage to CHANGE how you habitually THINK about things.

In Man's Search for Meaning (my favorite book ever), Viktor Frankl chronicles his experiences as a prisoner in Nazi concentration camps (including Auschwitz) during World War II.

In it he writes:

> *"We who lived in concentration camps can remember the men who walked through the huts comforting others, giving away their last piece of bread. They may have been few in number, but they offer sufficient proof that everything can be*

taken from a man but one thing, the ability to choose one's attitude in any given set of circumstances."

THE WAY YOU LOOK AT THINGS
AND THE THINGS YOU LOOK AT

In the Vietnam War, the future US senator and presidential nominee John McCain was captured and tortured.

Even under the worst conditions of what one human can do to another, he refused to be broken by the situation.

He chose how he was going to react and respond.

These both sum up the 3rd Universal Truth.

I have already mentioned in this book that the #1 skill you need to develop is courage.

The final Universal Truth expands upon this.

The third Universal Truth is all about having the courage to **CHANGE** how you habitually **THINK** about things.

I started this book with a quote from Seneca.

Seneca lived 2000 years ago and is known as one of the founders of Stoicism.

The Stoics taught that **it is our EMOTIONS**, that are our ultimate weakness.

Think about that.

It's our **EMOTIONS** that we need to control.

In other words, if we can change the way we look at things, the things we look at change.

Here's a question for you.

Can you control your emotions?

Or maybe a better question would be...

*...**DO** you control your emotions?*

Samurais trained themselves in this very thing.

Samurais are portrayed as incredibly skilled warriors.

And they certainly were.

But, in reality, they were much more than that.

What made Samurais truly special was not just their skills in battle.

It was their values away from battle.

It was their love of self-growth.

Samurais always had personal evolution top of mind.

Samurais would often talk about our **'perceiving eye'** and our **'observing eye'**.

The observing eye sees things as they are.

The perceiving eye, however, sees things as they could be.

For example...

Most people see things as they are.

A nasty comment from a lover.

A negative email from a boss.

A traffic jam when you are already late.

An expensive bill that you did not see coming.

Most people 'see these things as they are'.

A setback.

A hurdle.

A problem.

A challenge.

And therefore, most people automatically react with fear or anger or stress or anxiety.

However, the Samurais taught that we have a **choice** how we respond.

Sure, if we want, we can see things as they are (the observing eye).

HOWEVER, we can choose if we want to, to see things as they **COULD** be (the perceiving eye).

- IF YOU WANT -
Different Results
- YOU MUST HAVE -
Different Actions

In other words, Samurais taught themselves they have a **CHOICE** how a situation makes them react.

A choice.

This is important.

Because in **EVERY** situation life throws at us, we are presented with a **CHOICE.**

Take a moment to think about the #1 challenge you are going through right now.

What is the #1 thing that is causing you anxiety and stress right now?

Because by far the greatest gift you can give yourself, is the gift of understanding that you can **CHOOSE** how you **REACT & RESPOND** to whatever this thing is.

Many people go to the grave having spent their entire life ruled by their thoughts, and as a result, never even nearly fulfill their potential.

The first step of any reinvention is having the ability to look at things and realize that you have a **CHOICE** of how you can react and respond.

You are **NOT** your thoughts.

You are simply an **OBSERVER** of your thoughts.

Read that again.

This is not cute wordplay.

There is a big difference between the two statements.

Understanding that you are not controlled by your thoughts is (for many) a fundamental shift in thinking that is needed to start the reinvention process.

WE Repeat WHAT WE DON'T Repair

Or to put it another way:

You rule your mind.

Your mind does not rule you.

This is so important, so let's expand upon this a bit more.

Think about this…

…how you react to something is a **LEARNED** response.

What does that mean?

It means that when you think about a challenge in your life, the **AUTOMATIC** response you have to it (which is probably fear or anger or stress or depression) is a LEARNED response.

You were **NOT** born with that automatic response.

In fact, we are all born with only two fears.

The fear of loud noises and the fear of being dropped.

EVERY OTHER FEAR IS LEARNED.

So, by definition, when you think about a particular challenge that you are going through, it's important to realize you have **LEARNED** to react in the way you currently are.

Therefore, if you have **LEARNED** to react and respond in a certain way...

...you can **LEARN** to react and respond in a different way.

Make sense?

In other words, instead of AUTOMATICALLY reacting and responding to something in a way that HARMS you...

...you can **CHOOSE** to react and respond to something in a way that **SERVES** you.

Or to put it another way, if you change the way you look at things, the things you look at change.

This is the start of **GROWTH.**

Buddha said it best.

> He once said, " *Nothing can harm you more than your own unguarded thoughts."*

This is one of my favorite quotes.

I love how simple yet how powerful the words are.

Spend a few minutes **REALLY** thinking about these words...

> *"Nothing can harm you more than your own unguarded thoughts."*

Let me ask you, what are your own unguarded thoughts?

When you are laying in bed, when you look in the mirror, when you think about your life, what are those unguarded thoughts you have?

The impediment to action, ADVANCED ACTIONS. What stands in the way, BECOMES THE WAY.

Those secret, private thoughts that dance around inside your head.

What do you tell yourself?

Be honest.

Did you know, 99% of your thoughts you had today, are exactly the same as the thoughts you had yesterday.

You are literally repeating the same thoughts day in, day out.

So how can you change if you are thinking the **EXACT** same thing day in, day out?

You can't.

You won't.

Dr Joe Dispenza teaches that 95% of who we are by the time we are 35 years old is a set of memorized emotions.

What does this mean?

This means that how you are running your life right now, in other words, your emotional reactions to things, is just like a computer program running automatically in the background.

In scientific terms this is known as neural plasticity (also known as neuroplasticity).

Just as how the grooves on a hill get deeper as more water flows down them, so it is with how our mind works.

The more we repeat the same thoughts, the more deep-rooted they become, until eventually they are our default operating system.

And for most people this program has been running forever.

You don't even think about it.

Most people never question how they emotionally respond to something.

Most people never think about ...*how they think!*

They just respond.

They just react.

And therein lays the first challenge to CHANGE.

If you are **UNAWARE** of something, how can you change it?

You can't.

Brianna Wiest says in her excellent book '101 Essays that will Change the way You Think' that *the root of human work is learning how to think.*

So therefore, the **FIRST** step in **ANY** change, is to get good at being **AWARE** of **HOW** you are reacting and responding to something.

In other words, you need to start to develop the ability to observe yourself.

IF SOMETHING IS

Hard

IT'S A CHANCE TO GET

Stronger

Maybe you already do this.

If so, great.

But here's the thing.

Most do not.

Which is why most people do not change.

Because the brutal reality is we will end up repeating what we don't repair.

Remember the Stoics teach us that it's our **EMOTIONS** that are our ultimate weakness.

It's important you know this.

It's our EMOTIONS we need to be aware of.

And therefore, if you truly want to change, we will have to be **CONSCIOUS** of our emotions in the first place.

You have to start to be **AWARE** of how something is making you respond.

I want to encourage you to start to think *'huh, this is interesting, this thing is making me feel this way'.*

And you observe with **NO** judgment.

The process of reinvention **STARTS** by becoming conscious of your unconscious self.

In other words, all **GREAT CHANGE STARTS** by becoming **AWARE** of your thoughts.

And if you can start to observe yourself, it means you can self-correct.

Would you agree?

SIGNIFICANT LASTING *change* DOES NOT TAKE *years*

PART 1: SUMMING UP

In Part 1 we have been talking about the WHAT.

WHAT do you need to get clear on to start the process of reinvention?

Let's sum up what we have discovered.

1. The first thing we established is that no one is coming to save you. Any change you want to make is going to be down to you and you only. Sure, you can get support (and I'd love to help you) but no one is going to do your push-ups for you.

2. We then discussed the importance of accepting your current situation voluntarily. No more blame. Wherever you are right now in your life, is where you are. Sure, it may not be ideal. In fact, it probably isn't. But you need to own it, before you can change it.

3. And finally, we looked at how you view challenges. Most people need to re-frame how they view challenges. Most people see a challenge as an annoyance or an obstacle. However, the path to reinvention begins when we understand that all obstacles are, simply, an opportunity to grow.

I could sum up these three concepts with one word.

Can you guess what it would be?

We discussed it earlier!

The word, of course, is...

...courage!

Remember, the #1 skill to develop is courage.

There IS a path out of from where you currently are.

There really is.

But this path STARTS by stopping dabbling in wanting to improve yourself and really committing to it.

That takes courage.

Courage is what connects your thoughts with action.

The enemy of courage is 'over-caution'.

> Jim Rohn said: *"Some people won't do anything in life as they are too cautious."*

The following poem by Denis Waitley sums this up perfectly.

> *"There was a very cautious man,*
> *Who never laughed or played.*
> *He never risked, he never tried,*
> *He never sang or prayed.*
> *And when one day he passed away,*
> *His insurance was denied,*
> *For since he never really lived,*
> *They claimed he never really died."*

Don't be like the person in this poem.

Don't waste your time looking back on what you've lost.

Move on, for life is not meant to be traveled backwards.

At some point you need to get active in your own rescue.

Now is the time.

You're ready!

PART TWO:

The HOW

Now it's time to pivot and focus on HOW to get your life in order.

How much longer are you going to wait?

How many more years are you going to burn?

In your heart, you know there is no more time to waste.

I'm sure you have had many fleeting moments of thinking *'yes, I can make a change'*, only for that feeling to disappear just as quickly as it arrived.

We've all felt like this.

We all question what we are capable of.

We all suffer from Imposter Syndrome.

We all feel we are not good enough.

We all have moments of thinking *'yes, I can do this!'* only for those positive thoughts to be replaced almost instantly, often just minutes later, with doubts and fears.

This is also known as being human.

However, despite feeling this way, it really is possible to go from where you are right now to where you want to be.

Guess what your biggest battle is going to be?

It's not fear.

It's not time.

It's procrastination.

Procrastination is going to be your biggest demon.

That's what's going to hold you back.

Because procrastination is what holds most people back.

So that's what we need to overcome.

And we can.

Just for a moment, I want you to allow yourself the luxury of imagining what things will be like when you finally push through your procrastination and perceived limitations and begin to take those baby steps to being that person you secretly desire to be.

Imagine how that will feel.

Hold on to this feeling, as fleeting as it may be. Because this will become your WHY (more on this in a moment.).

What I want to do now is share with you exactly how you can break free from your current circumstances and truly begin to create a life that is full of joy, purpose and passion.

No more constantly watching YouTube videos.

No more scrolling through your phone wasting time.

No more procrastination.

You've come this far. Are you ready to go a bit further?

"Come to the edge, he said. And he pushed them. And they flew."

A Chain of Red X's

So, how do we start to change?

Let me share with you something I learned from Jerry Seinfeld.

Seinfeld talks about when he started as a comedian.

He tells a great story that as a young comic he had a wall calendar in his kitchen.

And every day when he would write some new material, he would put a big red X through the particular date.

After a few days, the big red X's started to create a chain of X's.

And the more days Seinfeld wrote, the longer the chain of X's on his kitchen wall became.

However, if he missed a day, then the chain would be broken, and he would go back to day one.

Seinfeld discovered very quickly that he didn't like seeing these broken chains.

Instead, he became obsessed with seeing a big, continuous, long line of red X's on his calendar, as it made him feel he was accomplishing something.

And then all of a sudden, a funny thing happened.

After a few days, even if Seinfeld did NOT feel like writing, he would force himself to write *even for just a few minutes,* just so he could cross off that day's date on the calendar with his big, thick, red marker pen.

As simple as this may seem, *this very simple system of tiny, daily continuous improvements, is the key to completely transforming your life.*

The secret is to start SMALL.

And I mean REALLY small.

Almost EMBARRASSINGLY small!

So, how do we do this?

I'm glad you asked...

Introducing your Secret Weapon

Before I share with you something that is going to revolutionize your life (and yes, I know how dramatic that sounds) I want you and I to have an agreement.

I want you to read the following with an open mind.

Deal?

Please don't make any judgment until you have read all the following.

Because what I am about to share with you, I have only shared with a handful of others (mainly friends and a few students).

But in all cases, the results for those that implemented what I am about to share with you, have been life changing.

Yes, life changing.

What I am about to share with you is one of the best things I have done in my life.

I want to introduce you to having a DAILY LOG.

Your Daily Log

What is a Daily Log?

A Daily Log is a journal.

However, it is unique and specific for you.

Your Daily Log will be unique to your situation, your needs, your goals.

And it's important that your Daily Log is specific to you.

Because your Daily Log needs to excite you, to resonate with you, to emotionally push buttons within you, to trigger you.

This is why most journals that can be purchased do not really make much of a difference.

Because they are generic.

Napoleon Hills says in Think & Grow Rich that *'specific information is better than generic'.*

And this is true.

There is a reason a brain surgeon gets paid much more than a general practitioner.

Nothing of course wrong with being a general practitioner, but when we laser focus on something specific, we begin to see results FASTER rather than being a generalist.

Having your own specific Daily Log is the most effective, easy, and frankly enjoyable way to start the process of reinvention.

Now, a few things first.

I like to be old school.

By that, I mean I have a printed Daily Log.

Yes, good old-fashioned pen and paper.

This means I hand-write in my Daily Log every day.

I have experimented with having digital version I fill in online, but for me, the act of taking a pen in my hand and manually filling in my Daily Log in my own handwriting and checking boxes (who doesn't love checking boxes?!) makes the progress a lot more organic, effective and fun.

I started my Daily log in 2015.

Over the years I have continually tweaked and refined it.

The version I use now is very detailed and allows me to test and track everything.

From my health to my wealth, to what I have learned today, to anecdotes and words and wisdom and quotes I want to remember, to habits and goals and victories and mistakes. And that's just the tip of the iceberg.

However, right now as you read this, I want us to keep things really simple.

We are going to create a **VERY SIMPLE** Daily Log for you.

What I particulate **LOVE** about having a Daily Log, is allows me to have in **ONE PLACE** everything that I have learned over time.

In fact, to this day, most evenings I will pull out an old Daily Log, open it up on a random page, and spend a few minutes refreshing myself on what I had written that on day.

This allows me to not only continually be growing and learning, but due to constantly dipping into old Daily Logs, I find I **RETAIN** information a lot better.

Side Note: I get asked quite a lot by friends and colleagues how I seem to 'remember' a lot of things. For example, when I give a talk, I can often pull in a quote from someone, or an anecdote from somewhere else, or a book title, or something that someone once said.

My 'secret' to achieving this is having a Daily Log. Because I have one CENTRAL place in which I brain dump EVERYTHING, and then I don't need to 'worry' about 'where something is' as everything that has ever impacted and resonated with me is in my Daily Log.

And because my Daily Log is only full of things that mean something to me, constantly refreshing myself of what I have written seeps into my subconscious allowing me to retain and remember what I have written.

This helps me hugely on my continual journey to learn, grow and evolve.

One of my best habits, in fact probably my best habit, is I fill in my Daily Log every day. And it takes just minutes.

In his book Atomic Habits, James Clear says: *'Your outcomes are a lagging measure of your habits'.*

What this means, is the circumstances in your life right now are a result of your habits over the years.

So, if you want to change your outcomes, we need to look at your current habits first.

In other words, it's time to explore the things that you are doing, and indeed (just as importantly) the things that you are not doing.

Example of a Daily Log

Here's a question for you.

What do you think the #1 Rule of Personal Development is?

The answer is as follows:

The #1 Rule of Personal Development is understanding that there is a huge difference between **TALKING** about something and **DOING** something.

So many people like to talk the talk; however, the cold, stark reality is only a very small minority of people have the courage to ever **DO** something.

Filling in your own Daily Log is going to be this 'thing' that you are going to do.

Are you excited?

You should be!

Because having your own Daily Log is the most effective, easiest, and frankly, most enjoyable way to start to process of reinvention.

Most people find it difficult to continually motivate themselves, and that's why a Daily Log works so well.

Because your Daily Log is built upon tiny, microscopic, daily victories.

Even if you are having an awful day, battling with the world's worst procrastination (and I have certainly been there) anyone can commit to 60 seconds of doing 'something' if only to keep that red chain of X's going.

And please trust me on this, all is takes is a few days of those 'Red X's' and you will discover that there is a part of you that will want to keep this going.

The secret of a successful Daily Log is to keep it simple.

Let me share with you now an example of a simple Daily Log.

Now, I should mention I have **TWO** different Daily Logs that I use.

My 'main' Daily Log is more detailed than the one I am about to share with you.

However, I am intentionally wanting to share my 'simpler' one here.

I use this 'simpler' Daily Log when I travel as it contains less to complete than my 'main' Daily Log.

By the way, if you would like to use my simple Daily Log to get you started, no problem.

I'll explain in a bit how you can get your hands on a copy (for free).

However, long term, I would encourage you to have your **OWN** Daily Log created that is **SPECIFIC** (there's that word again) and personal to you.

And I'll come on to how to have your own Daily Log created and printed and sent direct to your door.

But for now I want to share with you an example of a Daily Log.

Now, as I have mentioned, I have two different Daily Logs.

This is my 'simpler' one, that has less to fill in every day (as I've mentioned, I use this version when I travel).

Every page in my Daily Log is identical.

And this 'simple' Daily Log takes me about 15 minutes a day to fill in.

As you will see I have numbered each section.

There are 18 sections that I fill in every day.

This may seem a lot, but a lot of the sections are simple 'check boxes'.

And the other sections often take less than 60 seconds to complete.

Let me show you how it looks and then we'll break it down and go through it.

Chris Farrell's Daily Log (the simple version!)

Date: 1	Sleep/energy when waking: 2
Quote: 3	

Top Priority for Today	Top Priority for Tomorrow
4	5

Habits/Daily Victories

Recite 16 Laws	Stretch	Strength	Gratitude Journal	1.5 lit water	Personal Growth
6	7	8	9	10	11

What is my WHY?

12

Conversation Grenade | Learn something interesting

13

Word / Language

14

3 Wins of the Day

15	16	17

Daily Self Improvement

18

55

So that's how each day in my Daily Log looks.

And I fill in each section every day.

Let me share with you exactly what each section is.

PLEASE NOTE: I've also made a short video course talking you through creating and using your Daily Log.

This video course is inside the Reinvent Membership Site, and you can access it by clicking on the link at the bottom of this page, or by visiting:

ProjectReinventYourself.com

So, let's look now at what each section in my Daily Log means.

Daily Log Sections

1: **Date**:
Self-explanatory!

2: **Sleep:**
I make a note of how many hours I slept and how I feel when I wake. Tired? Energized? etc

3: **Quote:**
Every day I write a quote that has impacted me. The quote can come from anywhere: something I heard, something I read etc. I will sometimes repeat the same quote for a few days to make sure I really remember it.

4: **Top Priority for Today:**
Again, self-explanatory. But it REALLY helps to have your most important task for the day written down in front of you.

5: **Top Priority for Tomorrow:**
Before I go to bed, I always fill this in. That means when I go to bed, I know what my top priority for the next day is. This is important as this priority will seep into your subconscious while you sleep so you are ready for it the next day when you wake.

6 - 11: **Habits/Daily Victories:**
In my 'simple' Daily Log I have 6 habits that I commit to every day. And just like we discussed earlier with Seinfeld and his Red X's, I

make a note of the number of Days in a row I have successfully completed each habit. If I miss a day, I go back to Day 1!

Here are my habits that I commit to every day.

- **Reciting my 16 Laws.** I have a series of laws that I have created over time that I say out loud every day to keep them top of mind (if you are interested in knowing what they are I have them listed in the Facebook Group).

- **Stretch.** Self-explanatory. I stretch first thing in the morning - every morning (no exception) for 5-10 minutes.

- **Strength.** I do some sort of strength exercises every day (even if it's just 20 push-ups at home).

- **Gratitude Journal.** I have a separate journal where I write a page a day of things I am grateful for. This is one of the best things I have done in my life! I don't over think what I write, I just open my journal and write for a few minutes of whatever I am grateful for at the moment of writing. don't worry if some of my 'what-I-am-grateful-for' sound ridiculous! Nobody is going to read this. From 'thank you that my knees work' to 'thank you that I have food in my fridge', anything goes! It's important **NOT** spend time 'thinking' about what to write. Instead, the whole idea of a gratitude journal is to have a continuous flow, a 'brain dump' if you like, of things you are appreciative for at the moment of writing.

- **Drink 1.5 liters of water.**

- **Personal Growth.** I make sure I do some sort of Self Development work every day (and I write my takeaways in section 18).

12: **What is my WHY?**

This is my overriding reason WHY I am doing everything that I am doing. Your WHY has really mean something to you. Don't just write something because it sounds 'nice'. Your WHY must be that ONE THING that when you think about it, it will light a fire underneath you to carry on, particularly when you are feeling tired, unmotivated, or despondent (which will happen).

13: **Conversation Grenade/Learn Something Interesting**.

This may sound a bit quirky, but every day I like to learn something that I think is interesting. Something that can be used as a 'conversation grenade' to generate interesting and sparkling conversation.

14: **Word/Language.**

I am a big believer in increasing our vocabulary and so I learn a new word, or an interesting expression, every day.

15 - 17: **3 Wins of the Day**.

At the end of each day, I list 3 victories of the day. These wins can be small, but it's important to take stock and acknowledge how you are continually 'moving forward'. By the end of the day, you want to be a tiny bit 'better' than you were this morning. Making a conscious note of '3 wins of the day' really helps to keep moving things forward.

18:   **Daily Self Improvement.**

This is an area where I fill in something that I read, or watched, or learned, in the subject of Personal Growth. The Quote that I write every day (in section 3) is often pulled from what I write in the Daily Self Improvement section.

Ok - so that's the theory!

Let me show you how a typical completed day now looks using the Daily Log.

Example of a completed Daily Log

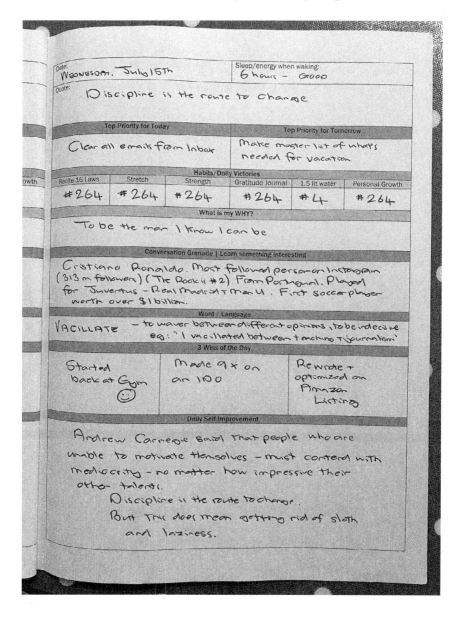

Date: WEDNESDAY, July 15th
Sleep/energy when waking: 6 hours – GOOD

Quote: Discipline is the route to change

Top Priority for Today
Clear all emails from Inbox

Top Priority for Tomorrow
Make master list of what's needed for vacation

Habits/Daily Victories

Recite 16 Laws	Stretch	Strength	Gratitude Journal	1.5 lit water	Personal Growth
#264	#264	#264	#264	#4	#264

What is my WHY?
To be the man I know I can be

Conversation Grenade | Learn something interesting
Cristiano Ronaldo. Most followed person on Instagram (313 m followers) (The Rock is #2) From Portugal. Played for Juventus – Real Madrid + Man U. First soccer player worth over $1 billion.

Word / Language
VACILLATE – to waver between different opinions, to be indecisive
eg: "I vacillated between teaching + journalism"

3 Wins of the Day

Started back at Gym ☺	Made 9 x on an 100	Rewrote + optimized on Amazon Listing

Daily Self Improvement
Andrew Carnegie said that people who are unable to motivate themselves – must contend with mediocrity – no matter how impressive their other talents.
    Discipline is the route to change.
    But this does mean getting rid of sloth and laziness.

#1 Rule of Personal Development

Earlier I shared with you the #1 Rule of Personal Development.

Let me remind you what it is.

The #1 Rule of Personal Development is understanding that there is a huge difference between TALKING and DOING.

In other words there is a world of difference between intellectually understanding something versus doing something about it.

Theory alone means nothing.

The world is full of armchair intellectuals who will read about something (such as having a Daily Log) - but will do nothing about it.

Don't be that person.

It's our BEHAVIOR that counts.

It's what we **DO** that matters.

It's our ACTIONS that define us.

Amelia Earhart once said, *"The most difficult thing is the decision to act."*

Execution is the most powerful weapon in your arsenal.

I don't care one bit about what someone SAYS they are going to do.

I hear it all the time (I'm sure you do, too) particularly in the online world. People SAY they are going to do this and do that. Blah, blah, blah. Talk means nothing.

It's what we **DO** that reveals our true character.

That's why a Daily Log is so powerful because a Daily Log is based on **DOING.**

Your Daily Log contains, literally, the baby steps of EXACTLY what you need to **DO** to move from where you currently are to where you want to be.

And here's the thing.

Changes that seem small, unimportant, and almost insignificant at first will compound into remarkable results if you are willing to stick at them.

Easy victories.

Tiny, daily wins.

Baby steps.

We've already talked about **courage** a few times in this book.

I have always been fascinated by courage.

I've always been attracted to books and stories about great leaders and visionaries who embraced courage and made huge changes.

However, one thing that I have discovered about courage, is that 'all' courage really is, is taking action.

That's it.

At the end of the day courage just means 'doing'.

Not 'thinking about', not 'watching a video about', not 'reading about', but **DOING**.

In the bible it says, '*Faith without works is dead*'.

This means that if you want to achieve something but are doing nothing about it, then it's not happening.

Making Your Daily Log Personal To You.

Let me add here, the beauty of having a Daily Log, is you can make it as personal as you want.

Remember, you have got to be excited to fill your Daily Log in.

This cannot be something that fills you with dread, or you feel obliged to complete it.

For example, you may have looked at my Daily Log and although this is my shorter version, you may be feeling right now that 18 areas to fill in every day is just too much (despite this only taking me about 15 minutes).

In this case, all you would do is create an even simpler version.

You can always add to it later.

Here is a version of a Daily Log I used to use that took me about 8 minutes a day to fill in.

An even shorter version of how your Daily Log could look!

Date:	
Quote:	

Top Priority for Today		Top Priority for Tomorrow
	Achieved? ☐ Yes ☐ No If no – why?	

3 Daily Habits		
Gratitude Journal	Stretch	Strength

What is my WHY?

3 Wins of the Day		

Daily Self Improvement

I've mentioned my 'simpler' Daily Log a few times now.

But you may like to know how my 'main' one looks.

This is the one that I use every day (except when I am traveling).

Now, please remember I have been doing this since 2015, and my Daily Log has evolved many, many times.

In fact, my current version is version 104!

Yes, I have tweaked and made changes to over 100 Daily Logs.

Please don't be put off by how detailed my current Daily Log looks.

It works perfectly for me, and I really enjoy filling it in every day.

I thought you may be interested to take a look.

My main Daily Log takes up 2 pages per day.

In total it takes me about 30 minutes across the day to fill in.

Here's what it looks like:

Chris Farrell's Main Daily Log - page 1

Date:						Get up time		Alarm		Energy when waking	

Quote:						How much did I EARN today?		**RUN HARD** Goal Date: Days Left: Goal:			

Goals – Financial for the next 3 months											
Month & how much:						Achieved?	☐ Yes	☐ No			
Month & how much:						Achieved?	☐ Yes	☐ No			
Month & how much:						Achieved?	☐ Yes	☐ No			

Habits/Daily Victories											
Recite my 16 Laws/PLM	Strength	Stretch/Yoga	Gratitude	Fill In Daily Log	1.5 lit water	Green Juice	Personal Development	Learn something interesting	Comedy/ Stand up	Brain health	

Goals – specific projects. $ PENALTY if not achieved.				
GOAL 1:	Deadline date		Days left?	Yes/$PENALTY ☐ Yes ☐ No/I owe $
GOAL 2:	Deadline date		Days left?	Yes/$PENALTY ☐ Yes ☐ No/I owe $

What did I do today to allow me to make money tonight?	*TODAY'S INTENTION*

What is my WHY that Makes Me Cry?	Today's Top Priority – EAT THAT FROG (i.e.do first!)
	☐Achieved?

Conversation Grenade / Anecdote / Comedic Story / Interesting	3 Wins of the Day
	1:
	2:
	3:

WDILT	
Social	Business

68

Chris Farrell's Main Daily Log - page 2

My Top 5 Highest Values (in no particular order)				
Financial Independence: Money/Business	**Health:** Mental/Physical	**Family:**	**Growth:** Learning/Habits	**Experiences:** Travel/Networking/Social/Adventures

NOTE: If I am doing something that is aligned to my **HIGHEST VALUES** it's a lot more likely I will ACHIEVE IT

8 Areas of LIFE	Daily Marks /10	What Did I Achieve Today in the 8 AREAS of LIFE?	Monthly Running Total
Spiritual: (LT) *(what did I LEARN today?)* Daily Self Improvement			
Education: (LT) *(what did I LEARN today – NON business)*			
Business: *(what did I LEARN/DO today? – FOR business)* * Online * Amazon / Other		What book am I reading/listening to this month?	
Relationships Significant Other / Family			
Wealth: (ET) *(what did I DO today to make $$ - be specific)*			
Social/Fun: Friends / Network / Experiences / Comedy		One thing I am doing that is new? What/when?	
Health: Exercise /Looks FOOD & ENERGY			
Contribution: How am I giving back?			

What is my TOP priority for tomorrow?	What could I have done better today — OR what did I LEARN about myself today — OR brutally honestly what one thing did I do to move my life forward today???

WORD/LANGUAGE:

End of Day	Master To Do List	Daily Self-improvement
☐ Fill in Daily Log ☐ Plan 2mora ☐ Read Daily Log ☐ Tidy Workspace ☐ 5 Year Journal Pomodoro		How much time did I waste today? How good did I feel today? How productive was I today?

By the end of the day I want to be **a tiny bit better** than I was this morning || What have I LEARNED today || Don't Waste Time || **Make Yourself Into Something** || You're not everything you could be and you KNOW it || The #1 skill to develop is **COURAGE**

Ok, so that's how my main Daily Log looks.

Now let's work on yours!

There really are only 2 steps.

1. Designing your Daily Log

2. Printing your Daily Log

Let's look at both.

STEP ONE: DESIGNING

The first thing when it comes to creating your own Daily Log is to get REALLY CLEAR on what you want to have in it.

How is it going to look?

What do you want to track?

Which habits would you like to list?

What do you want to include in yours?

The perfect Daily Log is personal to you.

For example, in mine (as you have seen) I have an area for a daily 'Conversation Grenade', but this may not be important to you.

I also like to learn a new word every day, but again, you may not care about this.

You may want more of an emphasis on finances, or family, or relationships, or contribution, or health.

This is why, as I mentioned earlier, a 'generic' journal does not really work.

The most effective Daily Log is one that is SPECIFIC to you.

In other words something that is aligned to your highest values.

(SIDE NOTE: Here's a little life secret for you: if you are doing something that is aligned to your values it's a lot more likely you will achieve it. Anytime we struggle to get something done it's because that thing is not aligned to our highest values.).

What I am really saying here is, your Daily Log must resonate with what you want to achieve in your life.

You want to wake up EXCITED to fill in your own Daily Log.

This should not be a chore!

I LOVE filling in my Daily Log every day!

And I've been doing it pretty much every day since 2015.

It really excites me to see my progress over time, to see what I have learned, to see how many days in a row I can keep my habits going (I have 6 daily habits I track in my 'simple' Daily Log, 11 daily in my main Daily Log).

It's very intoxicating!

So therefore, the next thing for us to do is to get really clear on what will be in your Daily Log.

Tip: Keep It Simple.

Here's a question for you.

What **ONE** thing would you like to commit to every day?

Don't over think it.

Say it out loud now.

Just one thing.

Maybe it's to drink a litre of water.

Maybe to stretch for a few minutes every morning.

Maybe it's to spend at least 10 minutes a day working on that book idea that you've been thinking about for a long time.

A great starting point for your Daily Log is to identify one habit that you would like to commit to.

You can always add more later.

So, what's that going to be?

In your heart, you already know something that you'd like to do every day that you are not currently doing.

> Could you go for a 15 minute walk every day?

> Could you cut back on sugar?

> Could you commit to finishing that course that you have not yet completed?

Identify just one thing.

And make that your habit.

To keep things really SIMPLE, if this is your first experience ever of doing something like this, I would suggest downloading my Daily Log so at least you have a template that you can start with.

And you can download my Daily Log in the Facebook Group (click on the link at the bottom of every page to join if you are not yet a member).

Print it out (you can have it bound if you like, I'll come onto that) and fill in at least a few of the sections every day.

You can leave any sections blank that do not resonate with you.

But I'd suggest at the very least committing every day to filling in these few sections:

- Quote
- Top Priority
- Personal Growth
- 3 Wins of the Day
- Daily Self Improvement

Filling in just the above few areas in the Daily Log will take you less than five minutes a day.

The one and only purpose with your Daily Log is to get you **DOING** something.

Not thinking about something.

Not talking about something.

But **DOING** something.

And once you start **DOING,** very quickly you will want to build upon the momentum.

Because you're not everything you could be and you know it.

But your Daily Log is going to start this process of making you into something.

Remember, small wins.

Incremental growth.

Baby steps.

This is how reinvention starts.

Now eventually of course you will want to get your own, specific Daily Log created.

Here's what I suggest.

Grab a piece of paper and draw out (by hand) what you want your Daily Log to look like.

This will just be a rough design.

Make a note of the sections you want to include.

If you are not sure, use mine as inspiration.

Make sure your Daily Log all fits on one page (so it's easy to print).

Then you have a choice.

If you have the skills, you can go to Google Docs or Word and design what you have just drawn.

Or what I did, was I went to Fiverr.com and got somebody to do it for me (cost me $10).

Just search for 'format document' at Fiverr.com and you will discover hundreds of designers who can make your design look fantastic!

One you have your Daily Log designed all you have to do is get it printed and bound.

STEP TWO: PRINTING

Once you have your Daily Log designed the next step is to print it.

As I've mentioned I would recommend printing and having a hard copy as opposed to having a digital version online.

Personally, I find there is something hugely gratifying and addictive about opening your Daily Log every day, starting on a new page, and seeing how you have done over time.

I use an amazing online printing service called DoxZoo.com

It's very simple to use.

Create a free account, upload your document, you can add a cover if you want, and choose the 'format' you want.

I always choose 'paperback book'.

Then DoxZoo print it on demand (you can have just one copy printed) and send it to you in the mail, all within a few days.

At the time of writing this for a Daily Log with 35 double sided pages (so 70 day's worth of a Daily Log) each Daily Log costs me about $8 (plus shipping).

That's about £6 in UK money.

$8/£6!!!

It's incredible value, and as soon as you place your order it will be printed and physically mailed to you.

Or of course you could visit a local printer (which is what I did before I discovered DoxZoo.com).

I must warn you, it's a FANTASTIC feeling when your brand new, shiny, and smart Daily Log arrives in the mail.

And over time you build up quite a collection!

A few years worth of my Daily Logs!

WRAPPING UP

Let's bring this to a close.

So many people want to make some sort of change in their life but have no idea where to start or what to do.

I'm here to tell you, that everything will change, if you create and start to use a Daily Log.

You are here because you want to make some changes in your life.

Discipline is the route to change.

That's why having a Daily Log is going to make all the difference.

At some point you need to get active in your own rescue.

How much longer are you going to wait?

Now is the time.

You're ready!

At some point you must put down reading about reinvention and act.

Another book is not the answer (not even this one!).

The right decisions and actions are.

How wonderful is it that if you so desire, you do not need to wait a single moment before starting to reinvent yourself.

In the end our life will always be shaped by our decisions.

And I'd like to invite you to make a decision now.

WHAT TO DO NOW

I hope you have enjoyed this (relatively) short read.

I created this book to share with you WHAT and HOW to start the process of reinvention.

If you would like to have support on your journey, I'd like to encourage you to join me at ProjectReinventYourself.com

DON'T
procrastinate

There you will find a hub of like-minded individuals all committed to learning, growing, and evolving.

In other words, reinventing.

You'll also have access many short video courses I have created that cover all aspects of reinventing.

From health, to wealth, to beating procrastination and overcoming depression, from building an on-and offline business, to creating passive income.

Project Reinvent Yourself is essentially a culmination of my passion and interest and 25+ years in the subject matter of growth, self-improvement, creating financial independence and living a life of meaning.

Project Reinvent Yourself is for you if:

- You have a deep longing for something different.
- Before another year passes you want to make a plan and get to work.
- You are not everything you could be, and you know it.

If this sounds like something you'd like to know a bit more about you can discover more here:

www.ProjectReinventYourself.com

To reinventing...
~ Chris Farrell

ABOUT CHRIS FARRELL

Chis Farrell is one of the most respected and successful online marketers in the industry today.

Chris's training products and websites have already helped tens of thousands of people create and grow their online business.

Chris has been in the entertainment and entrepreneurship industry for 25 years.

For 15 years Chris hosted the mid-morning drive show on London's #1 radio station as well as being the music/entertainment correspondent for Sky News/Sky TV.

In 2008, Chris relocated to Los Angeles and started a digital marketing business that within 3 years saw him become one of the most in-demand speakers in the world on the topic of business growth, marketing, and entrepreneurship.

In August 2010, Chris became one of the first online marketers to make over $1million in sales...in 24 hours, with a product he co-created called Affiliate Dot Com.

Chris is a popular in demand public speaker, having worked with and spoken on stage with Brian Tracy, the late Dr Stephen Covey, Gary Vaynerchuck, Robert Cialdini, Daymond John, and T Harv Eker, amongst others.

Chris is the co-founder of a talent/literary management and production company based in Los Angeles, representing creative talent, and influencers, in the fields of motion pictures, television, music, publishing, lifestyle branding and digital media.

Chris has also produced, written and presented podcasts and TV shows on topics including business, music, comedy, self-development and travel.

In 2018 Chris & his business partner launched FUNancial Freedom, aimed at teaching Children & Teens how to become financially smart.

In 2020/21 during lockdown, Chris finally got the time to focus on creating the reinvent brand which has been a lifelong ambition.

Originally from London, England, Chris has spent the last twenty years living between Los Angeles and London. Not literally in-between, as that would be in the Ocean...

Printed in Great Britain
by Amazon

80580351R00058